T0198777

His Hands Touched You First

JAYNE M. SMITH

WestBow Press books may be ordered through booksellers or by contacting:

WestBow Press
A Division of Thomas Nelson & Zondervan
1663 Liberty Drive
Bloomington, IN 47403
www.westbowpress.com
1 (866) 928-1240

Interior Image Credit: Dawn Harrison

Scripture taken from the King James Version of the Bible.

ISBN: 978-1-9736-7418-4 (sc)
ISBN: 978-1-9736-7419-1 (e)

Library of Congress Control Number: 2019913553

Print information available on the last page.

WestBow Press rev. date: 09/24/2019

For My Family

His Hands Touched You First

"For You created my inmost being: You knit me together in my mother's womb. I praise You because I am fearfully and wonderfully made."

Psalms 139: 13-14 New International Version (NIV)

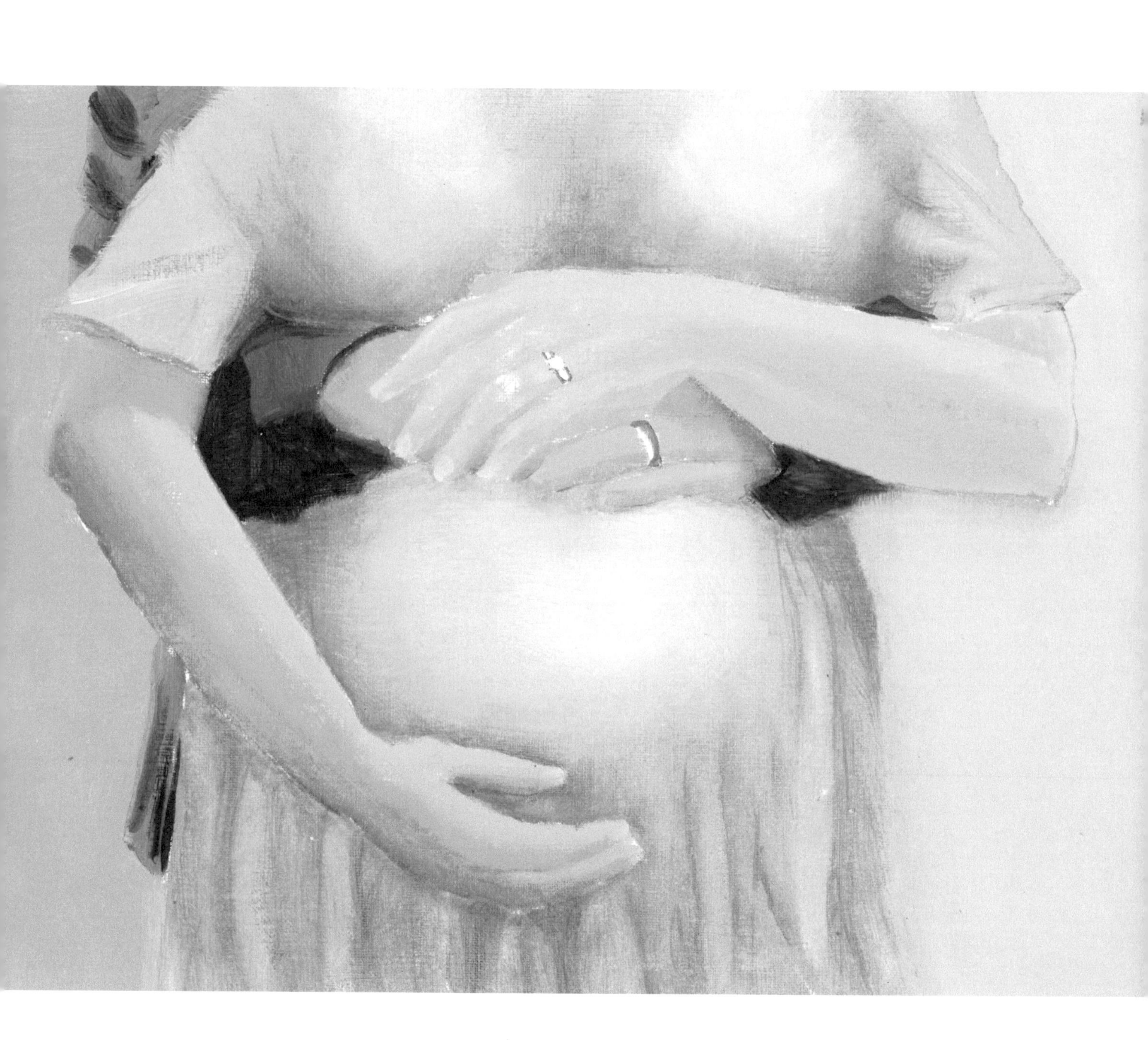

Hands wave, "Hello"

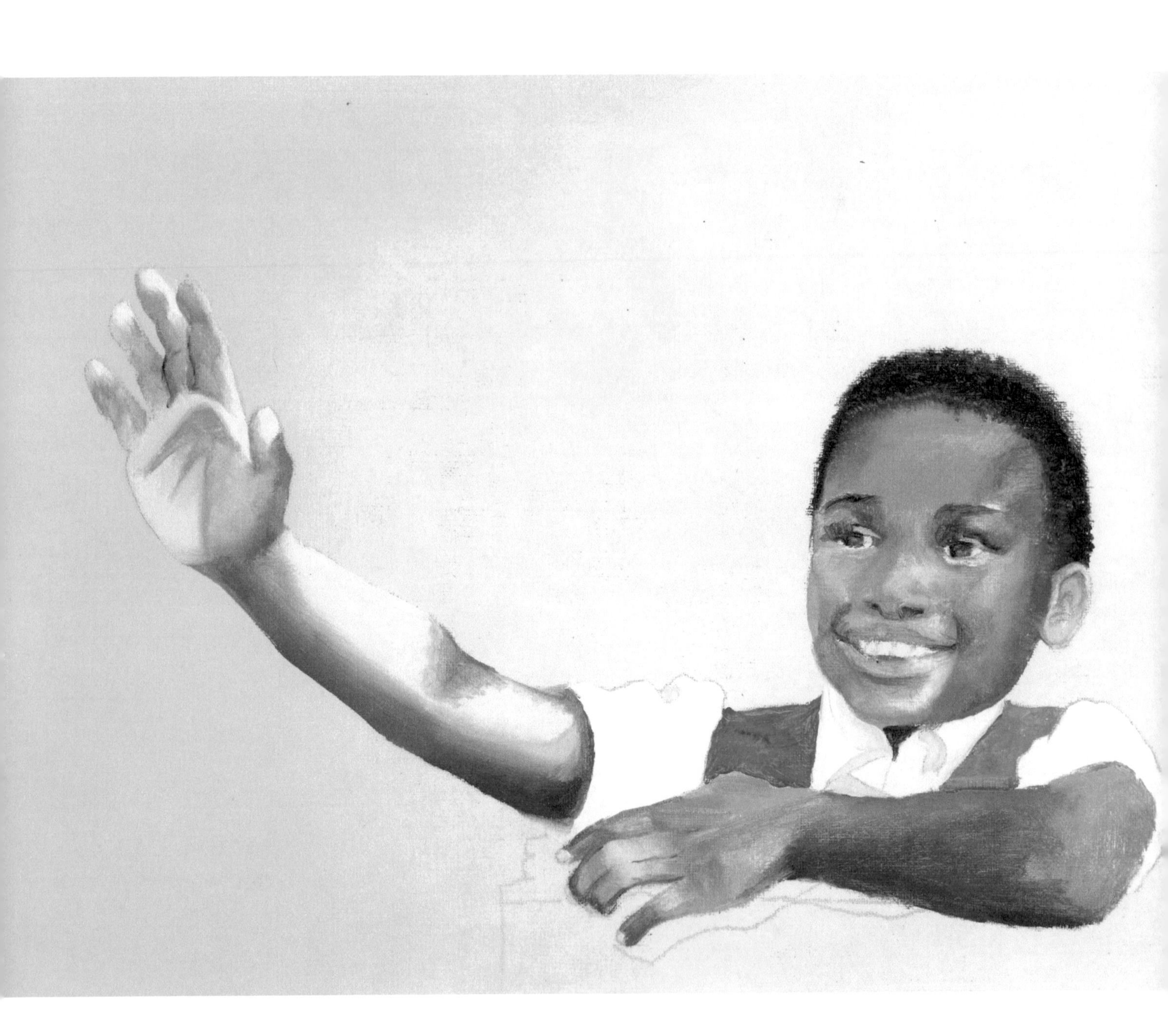

and we shake hands in greeting.

Our hands celebrate with applause.

High fives, low fives, pats on the back say, "well done."

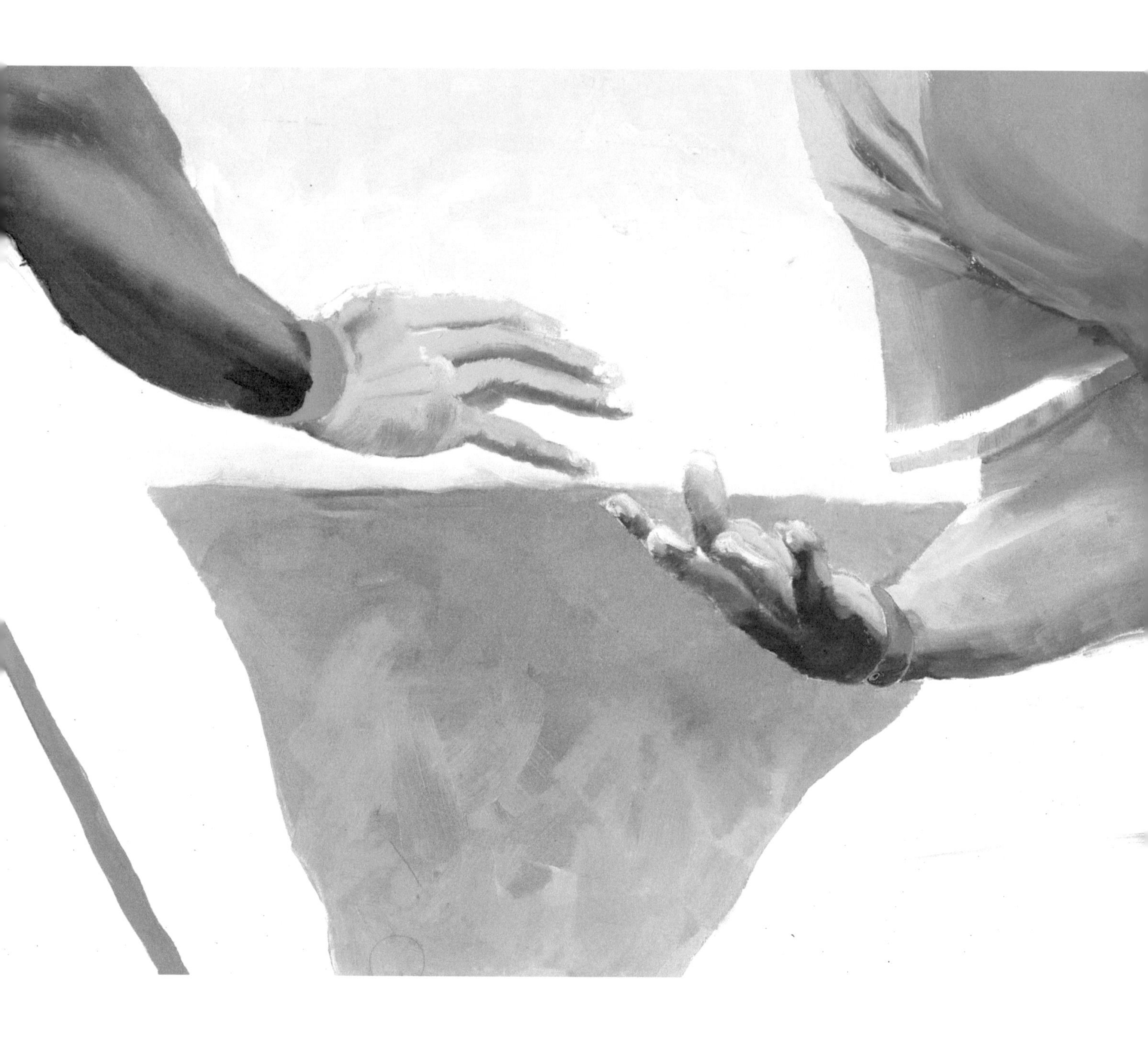

Dancing, snapping hands. Rhythms of clapping hands.

In quiet times; our hands give comfort,
wiping away tears, lending a hand up.

Gently rocking those we love. Picking flowers of gladness.

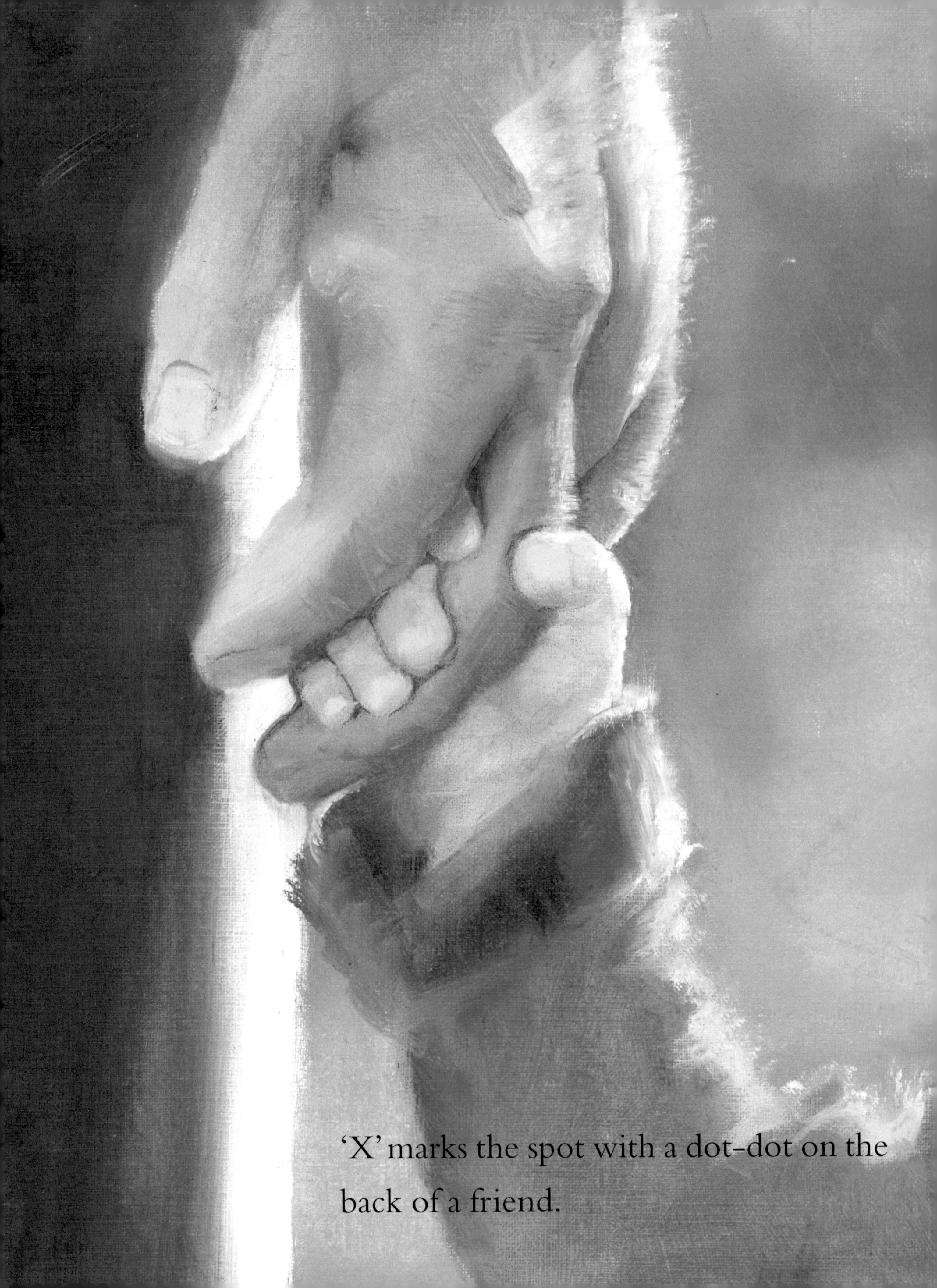

'X' marks the spot with a dot-dot on the back of a friend.

Hand holding in joy whilst our heart
skips a beat.

Attentively we stand with a salute of respect, our hands display our pledge of loyalty.

Allegiance is promised with our right hand covering our heart.

Spinner announces: "right hand on red, left hand on blue."

The hopscotch marker so expertly tossed. Cat's Cradle woven into another's hands.

We shoot hoops, tinkle the ivories, row the
boat, feel for fever,

write in our diary,

braid hair,

color and draw, build with our blocks, create shadow puppets.

"All with our miraculous hands."

"Tag you're it! siblings play, "Touched You Last"

At the shore we collect seashells, design sand castles; our hands digging damp, secret passageways.

Our hands speak sign language,
jet pilot language.

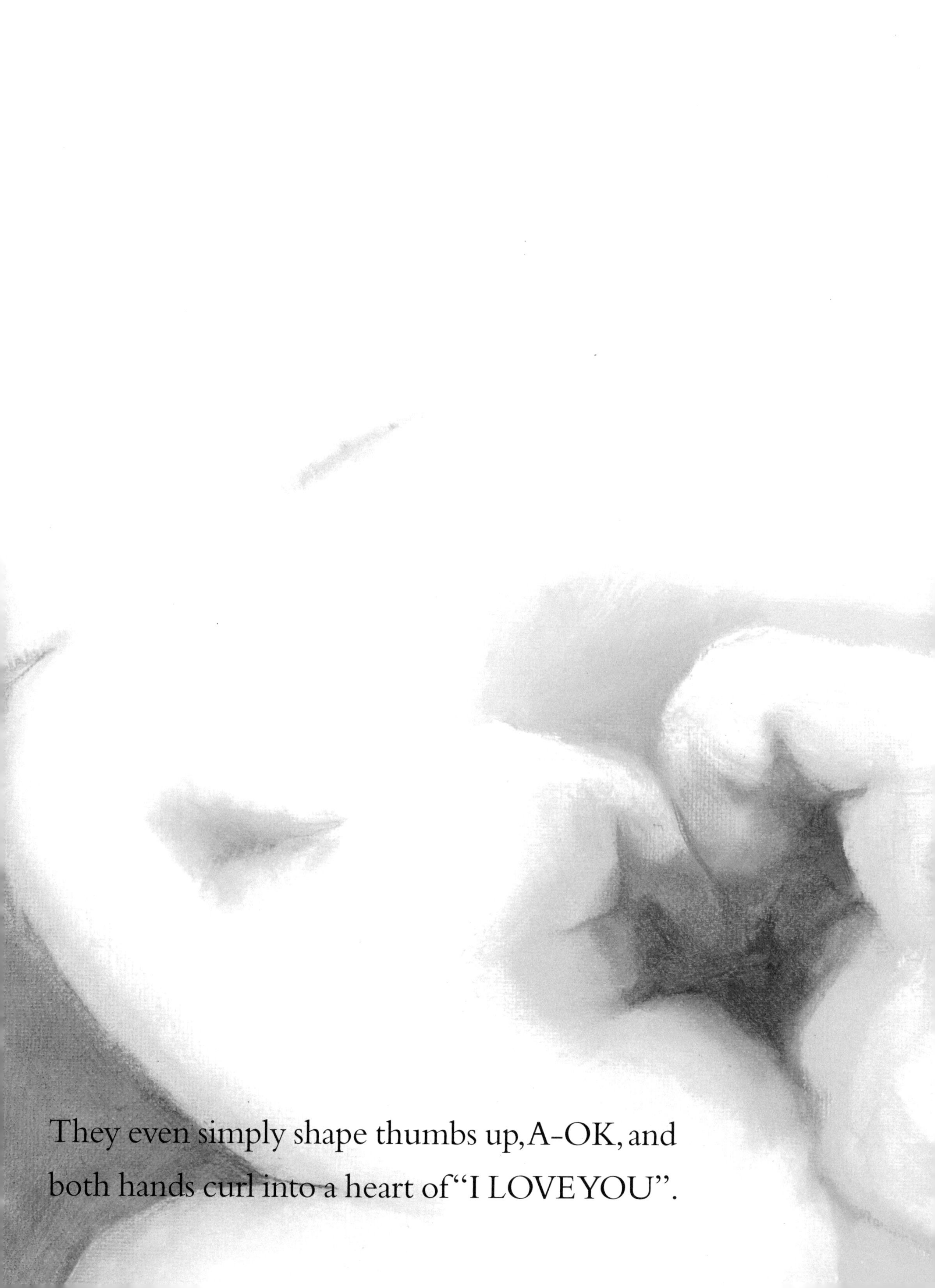

They even simply shape thumbs up, A-OK, and
both hands curl into a heart of "I LOVE YOU".

Our animals need our hands; walk the dog, feed the cat, groom the horse, catch the lizard,

pet the bunny.

Button, zip, snap, staple, paper-clip, open and close.

Busy hands sweep, scrub, shovel, rinse, rake, fold, tuck and polish.

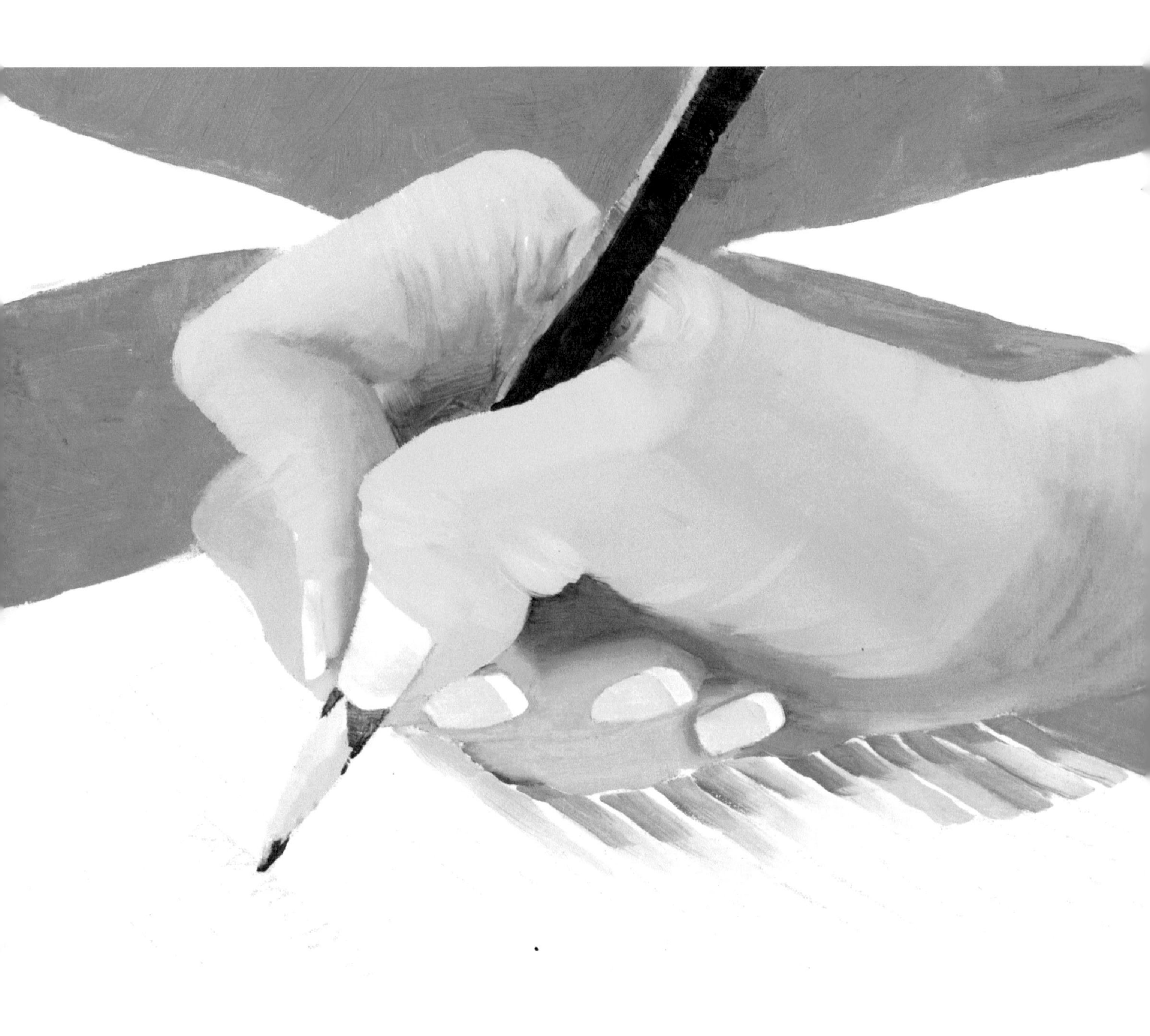

Our hands will learn to; "Sign Here", your signature is needed.

As you grow from start to end your hands tell your story within the hands of time.

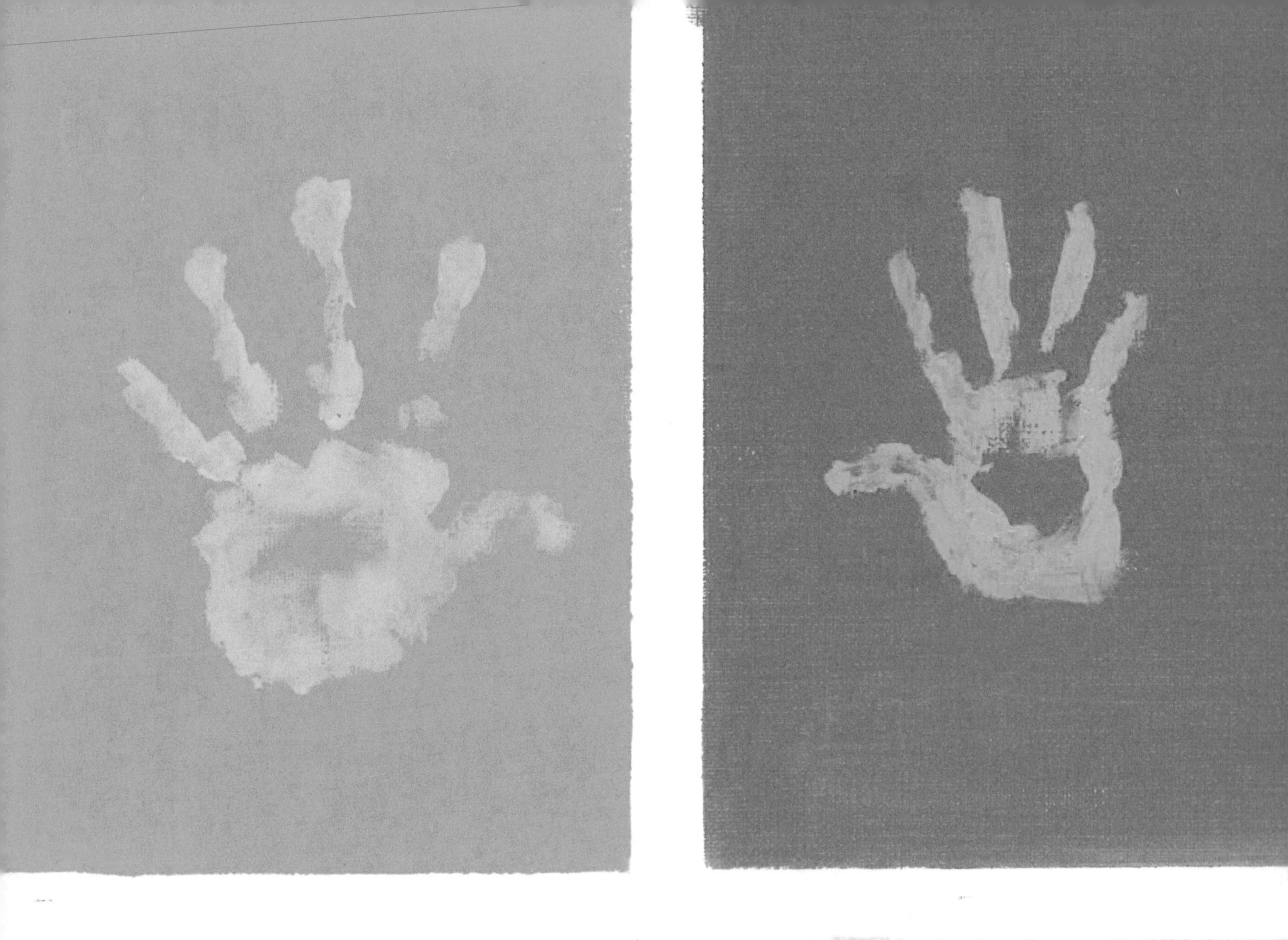

Handprints pressed into plaster and hearts for safe keeping.

Use your hands to blow kisses goodnight, goodbye, I'll miss you…always.

Hands joined in prayer and praise.

Lifted high, held open, touching gently, folded together.

Reach for Jesus' hands; hold on forever.

Remembering; His hands always guide and hold you.

"If I take the wings of the morning, and dwell in the uttermost parts of the sea; Even there shall thy hand lead me, and thy right hand shall hold me."

Psalms 139: 9-10 King James Version (KJV)

Printed in the United States
By Bookmasters